REVISED AND UPDATED

CELLS & LIFE

The Diversity of Life

From Single Cells to Multicellular Organisms

Robert Snedden

Heinemann Library

Chicago, Illinois

www.heinemannraintree.com

Visit our website to find out more information about Heinemann-Raintree books.

To order:

☎ Phone 888-454-2279

▢ Visit www.heinemannraintree.com to browse our catalog and order online.

© 2002, 2008 Heinemann Library
an imprint of Capstone Global Library, LLC
Chicago, Illinois

Designed by Kimberly R. Miracle and Betsy Wernert
Illustrations by Wooden Ark
Printed and bound in China by CTPS

12 11 10
10 9 8 7 6 5 4 3 2

New edition ISBNs: 978-1-4329-0031-1 (hardcover)
                     978-1-4329-0038-0 (paperback)

The Library of Congress has cataloged the first edition as follows:
Snedden, Robert.
  The diversity of life: from single cells to multicellular organisms/ Robert Snedden.
    v. cm. -- (Cells & life)
Includes index
Contents: A dazzling diversity -- What's in a name? -- Living kingdoms -- All together now -- Mutations -- Genetic drift -- Natural selection -- Adaptation -- Ripples in the gene pool -- Speciation -- Simple beginnings -- A tour of the kingdoms -- Protistans -- Fungi -- Plants -- Plant evolution -- Animals -- A brief history of life -- The end of the line -- The threat to diversity.
  ISBN 1-58810-673-X (HC) -- ISBN 1-58810-935-6 (Pbk.)
  1. Biological diversity--Juvenile literature. [1. Biological diversity] I. Title II. Series.
  QH541.15.B56 S64 2002
  570--dc21
                                2001008582

Acknowledgements

The Publishers would like to thank the following for permission to reproduce photographs: Corbis p. **16** (K. Willson); Digital Vision p. **5**; Garden Matters p. **12**, **21** (S. North); Garden & Wildlife Matters p. **43**; Getty Images p. **23** (Ralph Robinson); Link L. Bush p.**19**; Oxford Scientific Films pp. **6b** (T. Bernhard), **4**, **6a** (D Fleetham), **37** (B. Goodale), **13** (B. Kenmey), **35** (S. Meyers), **41** (C. Palek), **18** (N. Rosing), **7** (F. Schneidermeyer), **11** (M. Tibbles), **32** (B. Watts), **29** (I. West); Photodisc p. **36**; Science Photo Library pp. **42** (G. Bernard), **17**, **26**, **28** (J. Burgess), **33** (P. Goetgheluck), **27** (J. Howard); **9** (K. Lounatmaa), **25** (A. and H-F. Michler), **22** (G. Murti), **24** (G. Ochoki), **30** (J. C. Revy), **40** (S. Stammers), **31** (J. Watts), **15**; Survival Anglia p. **20** (J. B. Blossom); University of Florida p. **39** (David Dilcher and Ge Sun).

Cover photograph of a colored scanning electron micrograph of human blood showing red and white cells and platelets, reproduced with permission of National Cancer Institute/Photo Researchers, Inc.

Our thanks to Richard Fosbery for his comments in the preparation of this book, and also to Alexandra Clayton.

Every effort has been made to contact copyright holders of any material reproduced in this book.
Any omissions will be rectified in subsequent printings if notice is given to the Publisher.

Disclaimer

Contents

Some words are shown in bold, **like this**. You can find
the definitions for these words in the glossary.

A Dazzling Diversity

Diversity is the wealth of life. It is what gives life its power to survive. Several times in the Earth's long history, life has been dealt savage blows. At the end of the **Permian** era, 250 million years ago, 95 percent of the **species** then living on the Earth became extinct. Sixty-five million years ago, another catastrophe wiped out the dinosaurs and many marine creatures. Yet life bounced back and diversified once again. Today, life in a dazzling variety of shapes and sizes swarms the planet.

On land, rainforests contain the greatest concentrations of life's diversity. Coral reefs like this are the rainforests of the oceans. They teem with life, ranging from microscopic plankton to sharks.

Despite this incredible variety of life, all living things are remarkably similar at the most basic level. Virtually all life is made up of simple units called cells. All cells work in basically the same way, and they are all constructed from basically the same chemicals. Cells need energy, which they must obtain somehow from their surroundings. They also need raw materials to rebuild, repair, and reproduce themselves. Finally, all cells respond in some way to their environment.

Classifying living things

No one is sure how many millions of different species of organisms may be sharing this planet with us. New ones are being discovered and named all the time. An expedition to a region of Brazil in 2006 discovered 40 new species of plants and animals that were previously unknown, including a new bird and a tree rat. Every year, insects and smaller organisms are being added to the species list.

We can try to make sense of the tremendous variety of life by organizing the millions of living things into groups. Organization also enables us to find connections between living things that at first glance seem very different. The science of naming and identifying new organisms is called **taxonomy**.

The building blocks of taxonomy are species. A species is a group of organisms that can breed together to produce fertile offspring (offspring that are capable of reproducing). The African elephant and the bald eagle are species of animals, while the broad bean and the horse chestnut are species of plants.

Going up the scale, similar species are placed in a group called a **genus** (plural genera). All the species in a genus will have many features in common. Closely related genera are grouped into **families**, families into larger groups called **orders**, orders into **classes**, classes into **phyla**, and phyla into **kingdoms**. Kingdoms are the largest classification group. Animals and plants are the most familiar kingdoms, but as we shall see there are several others.

The tiger, *Panthera tigris*, is classified in the animal kingdom.

Pinning down the tiger

Looking at the classification of a single organism will help make the classification system more clear.

A tiger is an animal: it belongs to the kingdom Animalia. Within this kingdom, it is classified in the phylum Chordata (chordates) and the sub-phylum Vertebrata (vertebrates) because it has a bony vertebral column, or backbone. A tiger is a mammal (class Mammalia), a fur-covered vertebrate that feeds its young with breast milk, and it is a member of the order **Carnivora**, or carnivores. Tigers belong to the family Felidae (cats), genus *Panthera*, the big cats. Its species name is *tigris*.

Classification Plans

For a classification system to be useful, it must group the things being classified in a sensible way. For instance, if you were organizing the books in the library, a system where books were grouped according to the color of their covers would not be very useful when you wanted to find a book on a specific subject. To make the books easy to find, the classification system needs to be based on what is inside the book: its subject matter. For living things, the most useful classification system is based on how closely organisms are related.

How closely humans are related to each other depends on how long ago they had a common ancestor. If you have a brother or sister, your common ancestors are very recent: they are your parents. Cousins are less closely related, because their common ancestors are their grandparents (on their mother's or father's side of the family). In a similar way, closely related **species** have a relatively recent common ancestor. For less closely related species, the common ancestor is further in the past.

Dolphins and sharks look similar in many ways. A dolphin certainly looks more like a shark than like a deer or a sheep. But dolphins are much more closely related to hoofed mammals than they are to sharks. The apparent similarities between the two animals are because they have similar lifestyles and environments, rather than similar origins (see chart on page 44).

The barcode of life

To try to determine the relationships between species, scientists will compare different characteristics. In the past, they had to do this by looking at the anatomy of organisms (their structure) and at their physiology (how the different parts of the organism work).

The American robin, *Turdus migratorius*, is more closely related to British thrushes and blackbirds than to the British robin.

Carolus Linnaeus

An 18th-century Swedish naturalist, Carl von Linné (known by his Latin name of Carolus Linnaeus), created a system for naming and classifying organisms. Linnaeus's book *Systema Naturae* (1735) explained his system of classification for plants, animals, and **minerals**, and a later book created a more detailed classification for plants. Although many of the details of Linnaeus's system have been replaced, his system has remained the basis of modern **taxonomy**.

Today scientists have powerful tools at their disposal. They can compare organisms right down to the level of molecules. It is hoped that one day researchers will have an electronic handheld guide that can read a section of an organism's **DNA**, just like reading a barcode. This will tell the scientist exactly what species the organism is.

What's in a name?

The common names that we give the living things around us do not clearly identify them for scientific purposes. Common names are not very precise: robin, for instance, is the name for one bird in the United States and for an entirely different one in the United Kingdom. Also, robin is the common name in English; a French, Japanese, or Swedish speaker would use a different name. Most living things (such as many fungi) do not have a common name at all.

For biologists it is essential that there should be an internationally recognized system for naming organisms. The system used is called the **binomial nomenclature** system. *Binomial* means "two names." Each species has a first name that tells you its **genus** and a second name that identifies its species. The names are in Latin. In this binomial nomenclature, the American robin is called *Turdus migratorius*, while the British robin is called *Erithacus rubicola*.

Kingdoms and Domains

In the 18th century, Linnaeus proposed that the living world be divided into two **kingdoms**—animals and plants. As the microscope began to reveal more and more life forms that could not easily be placed in either kingdom, proposals were made for new divisions of life.

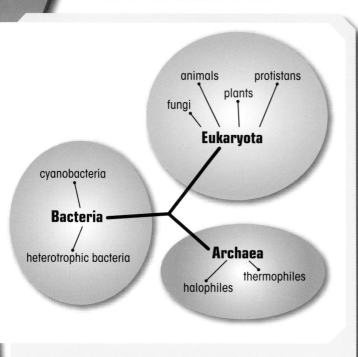

A diagram showing the three domains of life.

In 1959, ecologist Robert Whittaker suggested that there should be five kingdoms rather than two. Added to the plants and animals were fungi, **protistans** (single-celled organisms), and **bacteria**. In the 1970s, advances in molecular biology revealed that one group of organisms, the **archaea**, which had been classified as bacteria, were so different from all the rest that they really should be placed in their own kingdom. So we now have six kingdoms of life.

Archaea

The archaea, sometimes referred to as the archaebacteria, are single-celled organisms. They can be found living under some of the most extreme conditions on Earth, in places where no other organism could survive. Some live in hot springs or in extremely alkaline or acidic waters. Others are found near volcanic vents in the ocean floor at temperatures close to the boiling point, and in oil deposits deep underground.

Bacteria

Like the archaea, the bacteria are single-celled. The cells of both archaea and bacteria are simpler in form than the cells of other living things. They have no internal structures like other cells do—they lack a **nucleus** to hold their genetic material, for example. Cells without a nucleus are called **prokaryote** cells. The bacteria are a diverse group of organisms that are found in almost every part of the Earth. Some can make their own food using light energy, others use chemical energy. Many are essential decomposers of organic wastes.

Protistans

Most members of the protistans kingdom are single-celled organisms. The cells of protistans have smaller structures called **organelles** within them, including a nucleus that contains their genetic material. Cells that have a nucleus are called **eukaryote** cells. Protistans are sometimes divided into the plant-like **algae** that can make their own food; the animal-like **protozoa**, which consume other protistans; and the fungus-like slime molds.

Plantae

The plant kingdom is made up of a number of multi-celled eukaryote organisms. Plant cells contain **chloroplasts**. These organelles are where **photosynthesis** takes place. This is the process by which the plant manufactures its food using energy from sunlight. Organisms that can make their own food are called **autotrophs**. Many bacteria and protistans are also autotrophs. Plant cells have a thicker, rigid cell wall surrounding the cell membrane. Plants are important because they are the beginning of many food chains. Animals that eat plants are themselves eaten by other animals. Plants also produce oxygen, which is vital for the survival of most organisms, as a byproduct of photosynthesis.

Archaea thrive in extreme conditions, such as high temperatures or extreme salinity (saltiness). This photo shows the archaean Methanospirillum dividing. Magnification approx. x 29,000.

Domains of life

A recent proposal is that instead of dividing life into six kingdoms, it should be split into three domains. The archaea, previously included with the bacteria, would be given their own domain, since they are so different from everything else. The bacteria would form the second domain of prokaryotes, and the third domain would be made up of all the eukaryotes—the protistans, fungi, plants, and animals.

Fungi

Fungi are multi-celled and single-celled eukaryotes. The members of the fungi kingdom were for a long time included with the plants, but they are very different. Unlike plants, fungi cannot make their own food. They must consume other organisms, or their remains, to obtain the energy and nutrients they need. Organisms that do this are called **heterotrophs**. Fungi also have an outer cell wall, but it is made from a different substance than plant cell walls. Many fungi are important decomposers.

Animalia

The animals are multi-celled eukaryotes, and also heterotrophs. Some animals are plant eaters (**herbivores**), others eat other animals and are **carnivores**, and many other animals have a mixed diet and are **omnivores**. Animal cells differ from plant and fungi cells because they do not have an outer cell wall.

3

Populations and Genes

A **population** of living organisms is a group of individuals of the same **species** living within a given area. All the members of a population will basically look the same. Their bodies are built in the same way, their **organs** work in the same way, and their cells all work in the same way. In addition, the members will all behave in more or less the same way.

However, the individuals within a population are not all exactly the same. No two leopards, for instance, will have exactly the same spots. Some plants in a population might be better able to resist drought than others, and while most people can run, only a very few can run fast enough to compete in the Olympics. Wherever we look in the natural world we see populations with characteristics in common that identify them as a group, and individuals within these populations that differ from each other. Individuals in a species vary in almost every way that it is possible for them to vary. How do these endless variations arise?

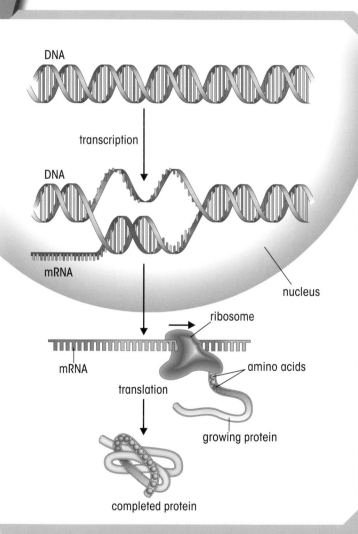

DNA molecules carry a code within their structure. One section of this code, the gene for a particular protein, is carried to **organelles** called ribosomes outside the **nucleus** by another molecule, mRNA. The ribosomes then assemble the protein according to the coded instructions.

DNA

The reason why all the members of a species are basically the same and yet individually different lies in a substance called **DNA** (deoxyribonucleic acid). DNA is found in every living cell in strands called chromosomes. It is like a chemical instruction manual. Built into its structure are coded instructions for making **proteins**. Proteins are the building blocks and workhorses of the cell. Some proteins are essential parts of the cell's structure. Others are **enzymes**, substances that control the endless flow of chemical reactions in the living cell. Each reaction that takes place in the cell has its own specific enzyme, and because the enzymes control the reactions, they effectively control the cell and the way it develops. Different combinations of enzymes, used in different ways, produce different characteristics in cells and in the organisms they are part of.

A segment of DNA that carries a protein-building instruction is called a **gene**. All of the individuals in a population will generally have the same number and types of genes. However, individuals within a population can have different versions of the same gene. Whether you have brown eyes or blue eyes depends on which versions of the genes controlling eye color you possess. There can be many varieties of each gene, so there is an astronomical number of ways that different versions of the thousands of genes can combine to produce a different mix of characteristics in each individual.

A green turtle (*Chelonia mydas*) laying her eggs. Each egg develops from a fertilized egg cell containing **genetic material** from both the female and the male.

Inherited genes

Organisms inherit their genes from their parents. Half the genes come from the father, half from the mother. In **sexual reproduction**, the male and female both produce special cells, the male and female sex cells, which contain half the normal number of chromosomes. A sex cell from the male and a sex cell from the female fuse (join together) to produce a new individual. This process is known as fertilization.

Fertilization is a random event. There is no way to determine which sex cell from a parent will successfully fuse with a sex cell from the other parent. The possible number of combinations that can arise from this shuffling of the genetic deck of cards is truly mind-boggling. There are 10^{600} possible gene combinations that can occur in humans. That is a 1 with 600 zeroes after it. If you consider that there are a mere 6 billion or so people alive today, you can see that it is highly unlikely that there is anyone anywhere who is just like you (unless of course you are an identical twin).

Mutations

Combinations of different **genes** might seem to offer all the variation a **population** could ever need. However, these are just new combinations of the genes that already exist. To explain the diversity of life, there needs to be some way in which new characteristics can arise and produce new types of organisms.

Almost every time a cell divides, the **DNA** it contains is copied perfectly. Sometimes, a mistake is made, and the DNA is altered in some way. The altered genes that result are called **mutations**.

Effects of mutations

We cannot predict when a mutation will appear. Nothing actually causes most mutations, they are simply random copying errors that occur when DNA is duplicated. However, each gene has its own mutation rate, which is the probability it will mutate during the copying of DNA. We can expect that a mutation will occur between every 100,000 and 1 million times a gene is copied. Such a slow rate means that in slow-breeding populations, such as humans, mutations are rarely seen. In a large, fast-reproducing population—such as some **bacteria** that can divide every 20 minutes in ideal conditions—there are plenty of chances for mutations and variations to arise.

A single mutation can cause a change in the color of an organism. The mutation could alter a gene that codes for an enzyme that controls the making of a particular pigment. In this bluebell (*Hyacinthoides nonscripta*) a mutation has resulted in white flowers.

Most mutations are harmful. A cell that has mutated genes usually dies because it cannot function properly. Sometimes a mutated cell survives in an organism. In most cases this will have little or no effect, since it is one cell among billions, although it could lead to the formation of a cancer. However, if a mutation occurs in a sex cell, there is a chance that it will be passed on to the next generation. Such mutations can cause serious problems. Sickle cell anemia is a genetic blood disease that is believed to have originally been produced by a mutation.

Close relations

Scientists can use mutations to establish how closely related species are to each other. There are some genes that are found in just about all living things. The genes that code for the enzymes involved in **respiration** are one example. The more closely related two species are, the more likely it is that these specific genes will be the same. For example, comparing humans and chimpanzees may show no differences at all in the structure of one of these genes. However, a gene that codes for one of these **enzymes** in mushrooms has up to 50 or more differences when compared to its equivalent in humans. What this tells us is that humans and chimps shared a common ancestor fairly recently, perhaps within the last few million years, but that the lines of ancestry that gave rise to humans and mushrooms went their separate ways hundreds of millions of years ago.

Some mutations are neutral: they have neither a good nor a bad effect. On very rare occasions, a mutation can be positive, and give an organism an advantage over the others in its population. If the organism with a mutation can pass this benefit on to its offspring, they will also gain this advantage. The mutation will gradually become more common, until after many generations, most members of the **species** will have it. This is the basis of **evolution**.

It is possible to use the average mutation rate to determine roughly when the common ancestor of two species lived. Neutral mutations, those that have no effect on survival, occur in the DNA at a regular rate, like the ticking of a molecular clock. Counting back the ticks allows scientists to calculate roughly when a specific species appeared. Results from one such study suggest that raccoons, giant pandas, and bears had a common ancestor that lived roughly 40 million years ago.

The red panda looks like a close relative of the giant panda, but gene studies have shown that it is closer to the raccoon. All had a common ancestor, however, that lived 40 million years ago.

Darwin's Great Idea

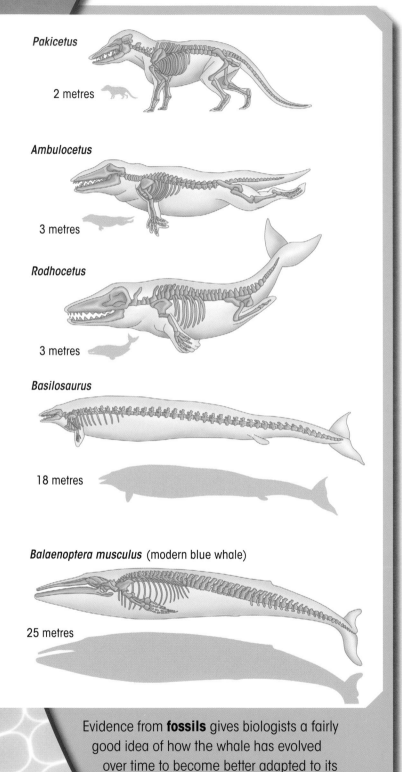

Pakicetus

2 metres

Ambulocetus

3 metres

Rodhocetus

3 metres

Basilosaurus

18 metres

Balaenoptera musculus (modern blue whale)

25 metres

Evidence from **fossils** gives biologists a fairly good idea of how the whale has evolved over time to become better adapted to its environment and lifestyle.

We have seen that **mutations**, random changes in the **genes**, can on rare occasions result in changes that are beneficial to an organism. Such mutations are important parts of the process of **evolution**, by which **species** change and adapt over time. But how exactly do genetic changes act to change a whole **population**?

No matter how successful an organism becomes, it is going to come up against challenges to its survival. For example, a population that is successful and reproduces rapidly will eventually run out of space and food if it isn't controlled in some way. If the population increases beyond the ability of the environment to sustain it, the individuals in the population will have to compete with each other for space, food, and the chance to breed.

Although all the members of the population have the same types of genes, we have seen that there is variety within those genes. Those individuals best equipped to survive in their environment are the ones that are most likely to produce offspring. A mutation that is beneficial is one that gives an advantage in the competition for resources.

For example, a plant-eating population of animals might be well-adapted to its environment. If a new predator moves into the area, those members of the population best adapted to deal with it will be the ones most likely to survive and reproduce. A beneficial mutation in this situation might be one that helps an individual to run faster. Over time all of the population will become faster runners, because the slower animals will be killed by the predators before they can reproduce.

What this means is that those genes that give the greatest advantage will increase in the population, while those that leave the individual disadvantaged will decrease. The individuals that possess beneficial genes are more likely to reproduce successfully. This process is known as natural selection.

Charles Darwin first began to develop his theory of natural selection during a voyage around the world on the survey ship HMS *Beagle*.

Natural selection

The theory of evolution by natural selection was first introduced by Charles Darwin, and independently by Alfred Russel Wallace, in the 19th century. Darwin saw that populations in nature have the ability to reproduce and increase their numbers over time. Indeed, more offspring are produced than will survive to reproduce. Darwin was inspired by reading *An Essay on the Principle of Population* by Thomas Malthus. Malthus argued that the human population could not keep increasing in size forever, because sooner or later it would become unable to feed itself. The size of the population would eventually be controlled by famine, disease, or war.

Darwin had the idea of applying Malthus's ideas to other organisms. He realized that other living things also have to compete for resources, both with other organisms and with members of their own species. Within a specific population there are a range of characteristics, some of which are better than others at helping the individual to survive and reproduce. A population made up of such diverse individuals has the potential to evolve. This is possible because those organisms that have the greatest likelihood of surviving have the greatest chance of reproducing. No matter how small an advantage might be, it will eventually be selected in favor of other characteristics. Natural selection, in other words, is simply what results from the differences between individuals. Some will survive to reproduce because they are better suited to their environment. This is sometimes called the survival of the fittest.

Because Darwin knew nothing of genetics, he had no idea of how these variations between individuals might have begun. Just about the time Darwin was presenting his ideas, an Austrian monk called Gregor Mendel was performing experiments with pea plants that would become the foundations of the modern science of genetics. Unfortunately, Mendel's work was overlooked until twelve years after Darwin's death.

Adaptation

The changes that occur in **populations** due to natural selection are called adaptations. A population adapts to its environment in response to an ever-changing series of pressures, such as changes in climate and competition from other organisms. The patterns of stripes on a tiger are an adaptation that allows it to get close to its prey without being seen; the long legs of an antelope are an adaptation that gives it the best chance of escape from a predator; the spines on a cactus are an adaptation that prevents thirsty animals from stealing the plant's stored water.

Mimicry

One of the best examples of adaptation at work is mimicry. Some organisms imitate the color or appearance of **species** that taste bad or are even hazardous to predators. Hoverflies are an example of this kind of adaptation. Hoverflies have evolved to look like wasps or bees. The hoverfly has no sting, but a predator thinks twice before attacking, giving the hoverfly more chance to escape from being eaten. The idea is that natural selection has been at work here, with birds in the role of selectors. Those hoverflies that looked least like wasps or bees were eaten, while those that looked most like them were not. The genetic makeup of the hoverfly population gradually shifted to favor the mimics.

Adaptive radiation

The adaptations that we see in living organisms are largely determined by the type of environment they live in. Many new species can evolve when individuals of a single ancestral population spread out to take advantage of new habitats. This process is known as **adaptive radiation**.

One example of adaptive radiation occurs when a small population reaches an isolated habitat, such as a remote island, and over time adapts to take advantage of all the habitats on the island.

This hoverfly (*Volucella inanis*) has no sting and presents no danger to predators. However, its wasp-like appearance deters predators from trying to eat it. Magnification approx. x 40.

1. Geospiza magnirostris.
2. Geospiza fortis.
3. Geospiza parvula.
4. Certhidea olivacea.

Darwin's drawing showing the different beak shapes of the Galapagos finches.

Darwin's finches

When Charles Darwin was a young man, he sailed around the world as the geologist and naturalist on the survey ship, HMS *Beagle*. During the voyage the *Beagle* visited the Galapagos Islands, where Darwin observed one of the most famous examples of adaptive radiation.

There are 13 species of finch on the Galapagos Islands, all similar but each with a specific adaptation. One species has a large, strong bill that is adapted for cracking seeds, another has a slender bill, adapted for probing for insects. One species has even learned to use a cactus spine as a probe to reach insects such as termites hiding in tree bark.

Darwin suggested that the different types of finches had arisen through adaptive radiation. There are no other bird species on the islands to compete with the finches, so they have taken on the roles that in other places are filled by birds such as woodpeckers and warblers. Darwin guessed that one species of finch colonized the islands thousands of years ago, and gave rise to the variety of species that exist there now.

Another form of adaptive radiation occurs when the dominant species, or group of species, in an area becomes extinct for some reason. Probably the best known example of this occurred about 65 million years ago, at the end of the Cretaceous period. At this time dinosaurs were the dominant large animals on land. Then some global event, maybe a large **asteroid** crashing into the Earth, led to the disappearance of dinosaurs. Their place as the dominant large animals was taken by mammals. Mammals underwent a spectacular process of expansion into different environments.

Genes in Populations

All the different varieties of **genes** present in a **population** together make up its gene pool. The gene pool of a large population of varied individuals is large because it includes many variants of the different types of gene. However, a small population of individuals will have a smaller gene pool. This lack of diversity may make the population vulnerable to any changes in their environment.

The bottleneck effect

The bottleneck effect occurs when large numbers of a population are destroyed by some natural disaster. The result is that the genetic diversity of the population is reduced because its gene pool has been diminished. Which gene variations are lost is a matter of chance.

Inbreeding occurs when closely related individuals with many genes in common mate with one another. This is likely to occur in a population whose numbers have been reduced as a result of a bottleneck effect. Inbreeding can lead to all the members of a population having the same genes for particular characteristics. Once again variety is lost and the population becomes less able to adapt to changing circumstances.

The present-day population of cheetahs is descended from just a few survivors from the 19th century. The population has a very limited amount of genetic variation because they are descended from such a small number of ancestors.

An endangered **species** can find itself in big trouble because of the effects of bottlenecks and inbreeding. One example of these effects is the African cheetah. Roughly 10,000 years ago, cheetahs probably came close to extinction. The modern cheetah population is descended from only a few hundred individuals. Cheetah populations fell drastically again in the 19th century.

Although the numbers have now recovered, inbreeding has led to a situation where today's cheetahs all have a strikingly similar genetic makeup. One **mutation** that became established in the population affects fertility. Most male cheetahs have a low sperm count, and 70 percent of the sperm produced is abnormal. This means that there is a low reproduction rate, which threatens

Approximately 30,000 people in South Africa carry the gene for the inherited blood disease porphyria. Each one is descended from the Dutch couple Ariaantje and Gerrit Jansz.

the future survival of the species. Zoos that breed cheetahs keep records of the genetic history of each individual. They use this information to help avoid inbreeding as much as possible.

Founder effect

A specific type of the bottleneck effect is called the founder effect. The founder effect occurs when a few individuals leave the population and colonize a new environment or become isolated from it in some way. The gene variations of the new population will not be the same as those found in the population they have left. There is likely to be less genetic variety than there was in the original population, and this can lead to a high frequency of inherited disorders.

In the 1680s, Ariaantje and Gerrit Jansz emigrated from Holland to South Africa. Either Ariaantje or Gerrit suffered from a mild disease called porphyria. Porphyria is an inherited blood disease, and the gene for the disease was passed on to one or more of the couple's children. Today, more than 30,000 South Africans carry the porphyria gene. In every case that has been examined, it can be traced back to the Jansz couple—a remarkable example of the founder effect.

New Species

Natural selection and **mutations** both work to change the genetic makeup of a **population**. At what point do the changes become so great that the population becomes a separate **species**?

What is a species?

Individual members of a species can be very different. A person might be short and heavy with dark curly hair, or tall and thin with straight blond hair, yet both are obviously human. Members of a species can also look different at different stages in their lives. Think of the tadpole that becomes a frog, or the maggot that becomes a fly. Differences in body form can be so great that we cannot use physical characteristics as a means of defining a species.

Earlier we defined a species as a group of organisms that can interbreed to produce fertile offspring. Dogs have been selectively bred by humans over many centuries, so that there are now many different breeds. Yet all dogs are still members of the same species, because one breed can in theory mate with another, and the puppies they produce are capable of reproducing.

Isolation

A new species can arise if two populations of the same species living in different areas become isolated from each other. One way this can happen is if the two populations are separated from each other by a geographical obstacle. The isolated populations will begin to look and behave differently, because random genetic changes and natural selection will shape the populations differently in different habitats. Such isolated populations of a species are called sub-species, and they can still interbreed. Eventually, however, they will become so different that they will no longer be the same species. Even if the geographical barriers between them are removed, they will no longer be able to interbreed. They will have diverged and changed to such an extent that each population is now a new species in its own right.

An adult male eastern lowland gorilla (*Gorilla gorilla*). The eastern lowland and the highland gorilla live in different habitats and eat different food. With time they will probably diverge to become separate species.

Hybrids

Two species that are closely related to one another can sometimes interbreed. The offspring that result are called hybrids and are usually sterile (unable to reproduce). A mule (a cross between a male donkey and a female horse) is an example of a hybrid.

How many species?

No one has any idea how many multi-celled species are living on Earth. Scientists so far have named about 1.8 million. Guesses as to how many species remain to be discovered and named range from as little as 2 million to as many as 100 million. Roughly half of the named species are insects: they probably outnumber other species by 20 to 1. In 2000, a group of 40 scientists formed the All Species Foundation, whose intention is to catalog every single species, from microbes to mammals, within 25 years.

Barriers to breeding

Differences that evolve that prevent organisms from interbreeding with one another are called reproductive isolating mechanisms. Physical differences may make mating impossible. Behavioral differences can also prevent mating, such as if one population does not recognize another's mating ritual. In some cases, mating can take place, but the sex cells are not compatible and fertilization does not occur.

A Tour of the Kingdoms

We have looked at some of the ways in which organisms can change and diversify. Over millions of years these processes have resulted in the millions of different **species** that we see today. Now we can look more closely at the characteristics that distinguish each of the six **kingdoms**, and the variety within each of these kingdoms.

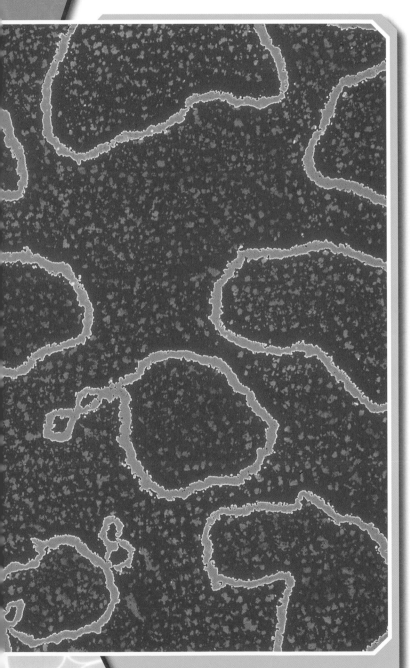

Plasmids in the cytoplasm of Escherichia coli. Magnification approx. x 80,000.

Bacteria

Bacteria are microscopic single-celled organisms that are rarely more than 0.0004 inches (0.01 millimeters) in length. They are found almost everywhere—in soil, air, and water, as well as on and in other living things. No one has any real idea how many bacteria species there might be, but one estimate is more than 1 billion. Four to five thousand species were found in a single gram of soil taken from a Norwegian forest. There are ten times as many bacteria cells in your body and on your skin as there are cells making you up. An estimated 99 percent of bacteria live in complex colonies called biofilms. These are made up of a number of species living together in a protective layer of slime.

Some bacteria are **autotrophs**, which means that they can manufacture their own food using sunlight and chemical energy. Other bacteria are **heterotrophs** and require a food source. Most bacteria are harmless, and some may even be beneficial, but there are a few that cause disease.

Each bacterium has an outer membrane, surrounded by a protective cell wall made up of a complex mixture of proteins, **lipids**, and sugars. Some bacteria also have a slime capsule around the cell wall. Inside the bacterial cell a large loop of **DNA**, sometimes called a bacterial chromosome, is attached to the cell membrane but not separated from the rest of the cell in a **nucleus**. Bacteria may also contain small, circular sections of DNA called **plasmids**. These plasmids can easily move from one bacterium to another, even across species. Passing plasmids from one to another allows bacteria to share immunity to **antibiotics**. This is one reason for the rapid spread of the drug-resistant superbugs that doctors are greatly concerned about.

Bacteria usually reproduce by dividing into two equal parts. This is called binary fission. Under ideal conditions some types of bacteria can divide every 20 minutes, but in most cases the limits of food and space mean that growth is much slower.

Archaea

In the 1970s, Carl Woese of the University of Illinois discovered that a group of organisms that had previously been classified as part of the bacteria kingdom were actually so different they needed their own category in the living world.

The **archaea** (or archeabacteria) are similar to the true bacteria in many ways. They are **prokaryotes** for instance, and reproduce by binary fission. However, archaea have some genes that are also found in **eukaryotes**, and more than half of their genes are totally unlike those found in any other life form. Because archaea are often found in the most inhospitable environments, they are also known as extremophiles.

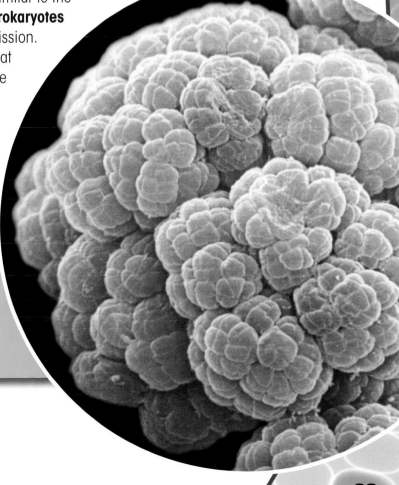

A colony of the archaean *Methanosarcina mazei*. These primitive organisms have unusual cell walls and membranes, and are methane producers.

Protistans

More than 200,000 **protistan species** have been named and described, and millions more are probably awaiting discovery. Most are microscopic, single-celled organisms. At first, they were roughly divided into three main groups: the plant-like **algae**, the animal-like **protozoans**, and the fungi-like water molds and slime molds.

However, as more and more has been discovered about protistans it has become more difficult to keep them in these simple groupings. There is more diversity among the protistans than there is in all the other **eukaryote** organisms—plants, animals, and fungi—combined. Many protistans are not closely related to each other at all. Some form colonies made up of many identical cells, while others, such as the seaweeds, are multi-cellular. They range in size from the 300-foot long (91 meter) giant kelp, a kind of seaweed, to **parasites**, such as the organism that causes malaria, which is small enough to invade the cells of other organisms.

Because they are eukaryotes, the **DNA** of protistans is separated from the rest of the cell **cytoplasm** inside a **nucleus**. They also possess other cell structures such as mitochondria (singular mitochondrion) where **respiration** (the process by which cells obtain energy from food) takes place. The cells of algae, like those of plants, contain **chloroplasts**, which is where **photosynthesis** occurs.

Giant kelp is found off the western coast of the United States. Dense forests of kelp grow every spring, then die in the winter.

Plant-like protistans

Most algae live in water, although a few live in damp places on land, such as the surface of moist soil, on damp rocks, and on tree trunks. Seaweeds are the most obvious algae in the oceans: in some areas giant kelp form underwater forests. However, tiny, single-celled algae are a much more important part of life in the oceans. These tiny plant-like organisms are collectively known as phytoplankton. Almost all living creatures in the ocean depend either directly or indirectly on phytoplankton for their food. Many marine animals graze on these tiny algae, and they are in turn eaten by other animals. Phytoplankton are the first link in the ocean **food chain**.

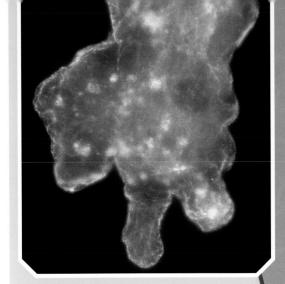

The single-celled, animal-like protistan *Amoeba proteus*. The finger-like projections of the cytoplasm are called pseudopodia ("false feet") and two can be seen on the left of this amoeba. Magnification approx. x 260.

Animal-like protistans

The animal-like protistans are sometimes known as protozoans, which means "first animals." Protozoans are found everywhere there is moisture, including the oceans and fresh water, in damp soil, and inside the moist interior of other organisms.

Like animals, protozoans are **heterotrophs**: they must eat food in order to live. They move actively through their environment in search of nutrition; some are grazers, some are predators, and some are parasites. **Amoebae** are protozoans that are very common in soil and water. They move around by forming projections called pseudopods ("false feet"). Most amoebae feed by completely surrounding their prey (usually smaller protozoans or algae) with pseudopodia and engulfing them. The digested prey is absorbed into the cell, and any indigestible material is expelled.

The Ciliophora, or ciliated protozoans, have numerous tiny hairlike structures called cilia on their surfaces. The cilia can move back and forth like thousands of tiny oars, pushing the protozoans through their watery environment. The cilia also pull food particles into the cell. Ciliophora prey on bacteria, algae, and on each other.

The sporozoans are parasitic protozoans that complete part of their life cycle inside other cells. The best-known example is *Plasmodium*, the organism that causes malaria. *Plasmodium* spends part of its life cycle in the *Anopheles* mosquito, and part in human liver and blood cells.

Fungus-like protistans

Plasmoidal slime molds are large, single cells fused together. Each cell has thousands of nuclei. Cellular slime molds usually exist as amoeba-like individuals. They will join together in a swarm in response to a chemical signal.

Fungi

The fungi include familiar organisms such as mushrooms, puffballs, and toadstools, as well as the single-celled yeasts and the true molds (see page 25 for water and slime molds). Unlike plants, fungi possess no chlorophyll in their cells, or any other way to make their own food. Many fungi feed on dead and decaying animals or plants, while others are **parasites**, feeding on living plants or animals. Some fungi live in or on plants in a **symbiotic** relationship, in which both organisms benefit from the association.

The **fossil** evidence that we have seems to show that fungi first appeared about 600 million years ago, roughly at the same time as plants were first colonizing the land. By about 460 million years ago, fungi and plants were forming partnerships. Roughly 100 million years or so later, the three great groups of fungi were established: the zygomycetes (molds), sac fungi (such as truffles), and the club fungi (mushrooms and toadstools).

Along with the **bacteria**, fungi are key members of the living world's clean-up squad. They are responsible for the decomposition (rotting) of once-living matter. This decomposition releases valuable nutrients for recycling, which would otherwise remain locked away in the bodies of dead organisms.

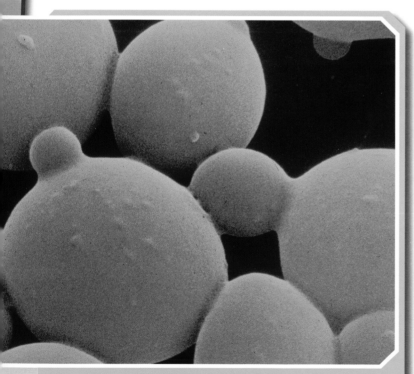

Yeast cells reproduce by budding. Budding is occurring in the two yeasts in the center of this picture. Magnification approx. x 6,000.

Fungal cells

Fungi are **eukaryotes**, and like plants they have cell walls. The wall of a fungal cell may contain cellulose, like that of a plant cell. It may also contain another **carbohydrate** called chitin, which is similar to cellulose but not found in plant cells. Chitin is the main material in the hard outer skeletons of insects and spiders.

Most fungi are composed of thin, microscopic filaments, called **hyphae**, that are capable of rapid growth. A network of hyphae spreading through a food source forms a **mycelium**, the body of a fungus. The hyphae form a complex system of microscopic tubes lined with **cytoplasm**. Although some **species** of fungus have incomplete cross walls dividing the hyphae into

Bracket fungi grow on dead tree trunks, but they can also be found on live trees whose bark has been damaged in some way. The hyphae are hidden from view, in the tree's bark, and the brackets are only produced when the fungi is about to reproduce.

cell-like compartments, the hyphae are not clearly divided up into individual cells. Each compartment may contain more than one **nucleus**, and cytoplasm is free to move from one compartment to another. This means that nutrients can flow freely through the mycelium.

Growing fungal hyphae produce **enzymes** that digest their food outside the body of the fungus. The fungus then absorbs the digested material. Fungi such as rots, which live on dead wood, can produce enzymes that break down the cellulose walls of the plant cells, but which have no effect on the chitin walls of the fungus.

Fungal reproduction

The mushrooms and toadstools seen above ground are actually the reproductive **organs** of fungi growing beneath the surface. The underside of a mushroom's cap is lined with gills (fine sheets of **tissue**), and here the fungus produces spores. These spores are the reproductive cells of the fungus. Fungi produce spores in large numbers. A melon-sized giant puffball can produce 70 trillion spores, each one of which can potentially give rise to a new mycelium. Spores are light enough to be carried away from the parent fungus by air currents. If a spore lands on a suitable food source, it will grow and form a new mycelium.

Mold fungi, like the ones that grow on decaying food, do not form mushroom-like reproductive structures. Instead, they send up vertical hyphae from the mycelium. These swell at the top to produce spores. In yeasts a cell produces a small growth, or bud, which gets larger and larger and eventually breaks away from the parent cell to become a new cell in its own right (see picture, page 26).

Spore production and budding are both forms of **asexual reproduction**. However, most fungi also have a sexual means of reproduction at some point in their life cycle. If the hyphae of two fungi of the same species meet, they may fuse together. This can result in a new mycelium that has **genetic material** from each of the fungi.

Plants

Plants make up a large and diverse group of organisms. They make their food through the process of **photosynthesis**. Photosynthesis involves capturing energy from sunlight and using it to build sugars from carbon dioxide (a gas in the air) and water. Because they can do this, plants have no need to move around in search of food and are adapted to a stationary lifestyle. This is reflected in the organization of a typical plant. Plants are typically made up of an above-ground shoot system for capturing light and making food, and a below-ground root system for absorbing water and **minerals** from the soil. Most plants are **vascular**: this means that they have internal, tube-like **tissues** that carry nutrients, water, and minerals to all parts of the plant.

Plant groups

Plants can be divided into four main **phyla** (also known as divisions). There are estimated to be more than 400,000 **species** of plants in the world, about 360,000 of which are **angiosperms**. The angiosperms are divided into two major **classes**. The **dicotyledons** produce seeds that contain an **embryo** plant with two seed leaves (called cotyledons). They have broad leaves with branched veins. Most herbaceous plants, such as lettuce and daisies, flowering shrubs, and trees and cacti are dicotyledons. The **monocotyledons** have seeds containing a single seed leaf. The mature plants have narrow leaves with straight parallel veins. Orchids, lilies, palms, and grasses, such as rice, wheat, and corn are all monocotyledons.

In this picture of a moss (*Polytrichum commune*), the yellow capsules and long stalks form the sporophytes. Mosses are members of the bryophyte division, one of the four main phyla in the plant kingdom.

Deep Green

At a conference in 1999, scientists gave the results of a six-year project called Deep Green. The goal of Deep Green was to organize and classify all the known species of green plants. They suggested that plants should be divided into three **kingdoms** rather than one, discovered the most primitive living flowering plant species, and possibly identified the mother of all green plant species.

The scientists put together evolutionary histories of flowering plants based on their **DNA** and then listed them in a rough timeline based on their **mutations**. They revealed that a rare tropical shrub called *Amborella*, found only in the South Pacific, is the closest living relative of the first flowering plant.

The Deep Green study also supported the idea that single-celled **algae** evolved into mosses at least 450 million years ago and became the first land plants. DNA data suggests that the green plants that first took root on land most resemble certain species of algae that are still abundant today.

Flowering plants evolved only about 135 million years ago—quite recently, in the history of life. Today they are by far the most widespread plant group on Earth. This example is an oak tree.

The **gymnosperms** are shrubs or trees that form so-called naked seeds. The most abundant of these plants are conifer trees, such as firs, spruces, redwoods, and pine trees. There are about 750 species of gymnosperms.

Ferns, of which there are roughly 12,000 species, have roots and stems but do not flower. They produce spores on the undersides of their leaf-like fronds.

The second largest plant division is the **bryophytes**. This division includes mosses, **liverworts**, and **hornworts**. The bryophytes are nonvascular. They are all low-growing, with leaf-like, stem-like, and root-like parts but none of the complex tissues found in flowering plants. There are roughly 19,000 bryophyte species.

Plant Evolution

DNA evidence suggests that the first **photosynthetic eukaryotes**, ancestors of the green plants, appeared in the Earth's oceans more than one billion years ago. Every plant in the world today is descended from green **algae** that lived along the Earth's ancient shores.

From water to land

The earliest evidence that plants colonized the land comes from **fossil** spores that are roughly 500 million years old, although plants may have appeared on land 200 million years earlier than this.

The earliest plants were similar to algae and **lichens**. Later plants developed simple structures that gave them some anchorage in their new environment. Eventually these developed into root systems. The above-ground shoots were at first little more than branched stems with spines.

Roughly 425 million years ago, the first **vascular** plants appeared. These had efficient transportation systems to carry water, dissolved minerals, and nutrients throughout the plant. These pipelines are made up of two types. Phloem cells carry sugars from the leaves to the rest of the plant, and xylem cells bring water and minerals up from the roots. The phloem and xylem running through leaves also act as a skeletal system that provides strength and allows for the growth of leaves that were bigger than would otherwise have been possible.

At some point plants evolved the ability to make **lignin**, a strong, waterproof material in their cell walls. The additional strength this gave allowed for the development of stems that could support leaves and position them in the best way to gather light.

Xylem vessels are modified cells that carry water around plants. Their walls are thickened by spiral bands of lignin (stained blue) that support the plant. Magnification approx. x 5,500.

Reproduction

As plants spread out across the land, their life cycles began to change. Algae, the plant-like **protistans**, need to have liquid water in order to reproduce. On land there is no guarantee that water will be available at any given time, and a stationary plant cannot move to search for water. In fact, the lack of water must have favored the development of plants with extensive root systems that could absorb as much water as possible from the soil. At some point in its life cycle the plant will form sex cells, but in flowering plants they do not need water to reproduce.

Flowering plants have developed two distinct types of sex cells. These are the female egg cells (found inside the ovules) and male sex cells (formed inside pollen). The **evolution** of lightweight pollen grains has allowed flowering plants to spread widely. Pollen grains allow the plant to get the male sex cells to the eggs without water being necessary.

In some groups of flowering plants the pollen is carried by the wind, but other plants evolved partnerships with animals, usually insects. In these partnerships the animal would visit the plant for food, and in return would carry pollen to other plants. Flowering plants evolved various large, colorful, scented flowers containing sugary nectar to attract insects and other animals.

Seeds have also contributed to the plant **kingdom's** successful colonizing of the land. Seeds are formed from the fertilized plant ovules. A seed contains an **embryo** plant inside a tough, waterproof seed coat that prevents it from drying out. The seed contains a supply of nutrients to give the new plant a good start in life.

The seeds of dandelions (*Taraxacum* species) are attached to tiny parachutes that help carry them away from the parent plant in a gust of wind.

Animals: Invertebrates

The most familiar of the animals—the fish, amphibians, reptiles, birds, and mammals—are vertebrates, animals with backbones. However, they form only a tiny part of the animal **kingdom**. More than two million **species** of animal have been identified, most of which are invertebrates, animals without backbones. Fewer than 50,000 species are classified as vertebrates.

Animal characteristics

All animals are multi-cellular. In most cases, the cells that make up an animal's body are divided into **tissues**, groups of similar cells that work together to perform a specific job, such as muscle tissue or nerve tissue. Groups of tissues are arranged together to form the **organs** of the animal, such as the heart and liver. All animals rely on consuming and digesting food for their nutrition. Because they need to find food sources, most animals are mobile for at least part of their life cycle.

Barnacles, such as this acorn barnacle (*Balanus balanoides*) feed by catching food particles carried past in the water, so they do not need to move around. However, young barnacles are different from adults, and swim around to find their food.

Invertebrates

Sponges (Porifera) are among the earliest and simplest of the animal groups. They live in the oceans or in fresh water. Unlike other animals, sponges do not have a mouth. Small holes or pores on the sponge draw water into a central cavity, then force it out through larger openings. Sponge **fossils** have been found from the **Precambrian** period, more than 550 million years ago.

Jellyfish and corals (Cnidaria) are a varied group of mostly marine animals that are armed with stinging cells. They probably evolved a few million years after the sponges.

Flatworms (Platyhelminthes) are simple animals whose bodies have just three layers of cells, making them generally long and flat. They include flatworms, tapeworms, and blood flukes.

Roundworms (Nematoda) are wormlike animals whose bodies are long and thread-like. There are more than 15,000 known species.

Starfish and sea urchins (Echinodermata) are ocean-dwelling animals that often have tough spiny skin. They date back more than 500 million years.

Mollusks (Mollusca) include snails, clams, mussels, oysters, squid, and octopus. They often have hard outer shells. There are more than 50,000 species.

Segmented worms (Annelida) include earthworms and their relatives, leeches, and a large number of marine worms known as polychaetes. Some live in the soil, some live in the oceans, and some are **parasites**. Their bodies are made up of separate segments.

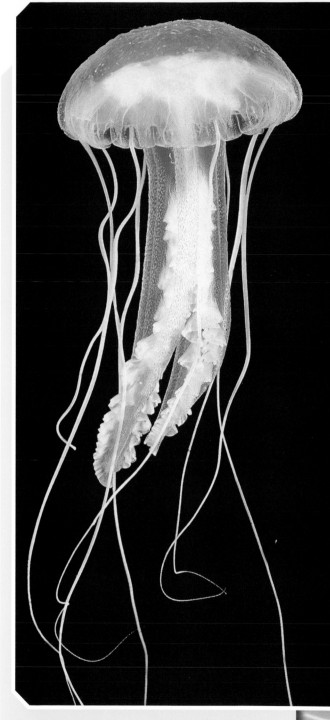

This jellyfish (*Pelaga noctiluca*) feeds by paralyzing its prey with tiny stinging cells from its eight tentacles.

Arthropods (Arthropoda) include insects, spiders, scorpions, and crustaceans (such as crabs and shrimp). Roughly 80 percent of animals are arthropods, and the majority of arthropods are insects. There are more insect species than all other animals combined. Arthropods have jointed limbs and a hard outer skeleton, or exoskeleton, which they shed at intervals as they grow.

Animals: Vertebrates

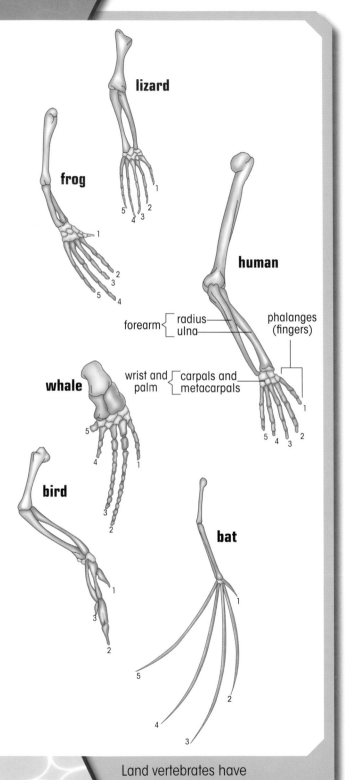

lizard

frog

human

1
2
3
4
5

1
2
3
5
4

whale

5
4
1

wrist and palm { carpals and metacarpals }

forearm { radius ulna }

phalanges (fingers)

5 4 3 2

1

bird

3
2
1

bat

1

5

2

4

3

Land vertebrates have characteristic pentadactyl (five-fingered) limbs. The limbs have evolved in different ways in different species.

Vertebrates have a long history on Earth—more than 500 million years. The first vertebrates were jawless fish, similar to today's hagfish and lampreys. **Fossils** of jawed vertebrates appeared roughly 100 million years later.

A vertebrate is distinguished from other animals by its backbone. This segmented column can be made of **cartilage** or bone and protects the spinal cord. The brain is protected inside a bony skull. Other features of vertebrates include a relatively well-developed brain, paired complex eyes, a muscular mouth, and a well-developed circulatory system with a heart.

Fish

There are three main fish **classes**: the jawless fish, the cartilaginous fish (fish whose skeleton is made of cartilage), and the bony fish. The jawless fish are the oldest vertebrates, as we have seen. The cartilaginous fish include sharks, skates, and rays. Instead of scales, their skin is covered in tiny, toothlike objects called **denticles**.

Of the 29,000 known **species** of fish, 96 percent are bony fish. Bony fish first evolved roughly 130 million years ago, but they dominate today's oceans. They come in a wide variety of forms and sizes, and live in a wide range of watery habitats.

Amphibians

Frogs, toads, and newts are the best-known amphibians. They spend part of their lives in water and part on land, and have a unique ability to breathe both on land and in the water. In water they breathe through their smooth, scaleless skin. For breathing on land, most amphibians have lungs.

Reptiles

Reptiles are cold-blooded animals and were the first of the true land-dwelling vertebrates, because they did not return to water to breed. The earliest fossil of a reptile is a tiny, lizard-like creature called *Petrolacosaurus* from nearly 350 million years ago. There are roughly 8,000 known modern reptiles, including crocodiles, lizards, snakes, and turtles. They have scaly skin and lay eggs with leathery shells.

Birds

Birds are land-dwelling animals that breathe through lungs and keep a constant body temperature. All have wings and feathers and most can fly. They have beaks for feeding, and lay eggs with hard shells. There are roughly 9,000 species. They probably evolved from small dinosaurs more than 200 million years ago.

Mammals

Mammals are more intelligent than other animals, and like birds they can keep their body temperature constant despite changes in the temperature of their surroundings. Nearly all mammals have hair or fur, and the young feed for the early part of their life on their mother's milk. There are roughly 5,000 mammal species, the large majority of which are **placental** mammals. Placental mammals produce live young, which are nourished in the mother's womb through a specialized **organ** called the placenta. Placental mammals range in size from shrews to whales and include dogs, cats, sheep, cattle, and humans.

Marsupials are the second largest mammal group. They include all of the pouched animals, such as opossums, kangaroos, and koalas. Their babies are born tiny and helpless, then grow and develop in the mother's pouch. The third group, the **monotremes**, are mammals that lay eggs rather than producing live young. The best-known monotreme is the duck-billed platypus.

A Brief History of Life

The planet Earth is roughly 4.6 billion years old. For the first 800 million years or so of its existence it was subjected to bombardments from giant meteorites. Volcanic eruptions and gases escaping from the hot surface of the young planet formed its early atmosphere. As the planet cooled and its crust solidified, roughly 4 billion years ago, torrential rains fell, creating the oceans.

The oldest traces of life that have been found are **bacteria**-like **organisms** roughly 3.5 billion years old. Almost certainly there would have been life even earlier than this—some think as early as the first solid crust. It is possible that life appeared again and again on the Earth, only to be wiped out by a catastrophe such as an asteroid impact and to reappear in another form. Eventually though, some pocket of life survived. Every organism alive on Earth today can trace its ancestry back to those survivors.

Earliest life

Evolution can't tell us how life first appeared. Evolution is only concerned with how life changed and evolved. The first cells were probably similar to the **archaea**. They found themselves in a harsh environment. There was no ozone layer to block the ultraviolet radiation from the sun, and this would have resulted in many **mutations** in the archaean **DNA**. These mutations would have been a factor in driving the evolution of these first cells. Many archaea today are found in conditions that are similar to those found on the early Earth, such as ocean-floor volcanic vents, and hot springs of more than 212 °F (100 °C).

No one is sure about the relationship between archaea and bacteria. They may have developed separately from a common ancestor soon after life began.

The changes in the atmosphere of our planet were important in establishing life on Earth.

Stromatolites are rock-like structures created from deposits trapped by photosynthetic bacteria. Stromatolite **fossils** have been found in rocks that are three billion years old.

A change in the atmosphere

Bacteria emerged that could harness the energy of the sun to make food through the process of **photosynthesis**. This allowed bacteria to tap into an unlimited source of energy for life. This was a major leap forward in the history of life. As oxygen, a byproduct of photosynthesis, slowly accumulated in the atmosphere over hundreds of millions of years, it had a twofold effect. One was that it accumulated in the upper atmosphere as ozone, blocking harmful UV radiation. The second was that organisms evolved a way of using it to release energy more efficiently than before from their food.

The first **eukaryotes** evolved from the archaea between 1.6 billion and 2 billion years ago. It took a long time for single-celled life to evolve into more complex, multi-cellular organisms. The best guess is that multi-celled life appeared 600–700 million years ago, perhaps when some early **protozoans** formed a colony that became a single organism similar to a present day sponge. It may have been an extraordinarily difficult step for life to take. Perhaps it was necessary for photosynthesis and **respiration** to evolve first. Thus equipped, life began to take off in a big way, spreading out and diversifying into all of the environments that the young Earth had to offer. Multi-celled life, plants, animals and fungi, took the stage.

An Explosion of Life

Our picture of the past is incomplete. Only those organisms with hard body parts that happened to be buried in just the right circumstances for **fossil** formation, and that happened to have been discovered by fossil hunters, play a part in this story. Scientists believe that fewer than 4 percent of the organisms that have lived have left a fossil record.

By the end of the **Precambrian** era, 570 million years ago, the world was rich in life, but we have no record of what that life was like. The fossil record for this period is extremely poor. We know that there were **protistans**, fungi, and animals, although there were no plants yet. Most of the major animal forms evolved for the first time in the seas of the **Cambrian** era that followed. Many of these early animal **species** probably lived in the sediments, rich in **organic** remains, that drifted down to the seafloor. These primitive animals were extraordinarily diverse.

The great diversification that took place roughly 530 million years ago is sometimes called the "big bang" of animal **evolution**, or the Cambrian explosion. The reasons for this outpouring of forms is not entirely clear, and some scientists would dispute that there was an explosion at all. Remember that we know very little of what was going on before this period.

One reason for the sudden diversity was probably competition. Animals were competing with each other as predators and prey and evolved new ways of attack and defense. Then, as now, the race between predator and prey was one of the greatest forces of evolution.

Hallucigenia
(an early echinoderm)

Vauxia
(a sponge)

Anomalocaris
(an early arthropod)

Olenoides
(a trilobite)

Dinomischus
(a primitive invertebrate)

Pikaia
(a primitive chordate)

Canadia
(a polychaete worm)

Reconstructions of some of the life forms that appeared during the Cambrian explosion (545–505 million years ago).

Colonizing the land

The Cambrian explosion took place entirely in the water. The land was lifeless and empty. By about 450 million years ago, some areas may have supported a few **lichens**, and on the margins of rivers there were probably green **algae**. Land plants may have developed from these freshwater algae.

Land animals

As plants began to colonize the land, animals followed. The earliest animal colonizers were **arthropods** such as spiders and millipedes. Then roughly 360 million years ago, new animals began to colonize the land—the **tetrapods**. These animals evolved from fish and diversified into the amphibians, reptiles, birds, and mammals we see today. However, like modern amphibians, the early tetrapods needed to return to the water to breed. To be true land animals, they had to develop a way to reproduce without water.

A fossil of the plant *Archaefructus liaoningensis*, currently the oldest flowering plant fossil known. It was found in China in rocks roughly 140 million years old. The plant does not have obvious flowers or fruits: the plant's seeds are contained in folded leaves.

This step came with the evolution of the reptiles. They laid eggs that were protected from drying out by a leathery shell. Inside the egg the developing **embryo** grows in its own "pool" protected by a membrane called the amnion. Because of this feature, reptiles and other land-dwelling animals that descended from them, the birds and mammals, are called **amniotes**. No longer dependent on staying near a water supply, the amniotes could spread out across the Earth.

Trilobites were a highly successful group of **arthropods**. For 300 million years, beginning in the **Cambrian** period, they lived in the ancient oceans. Then 250 million years ago, at the end of the Permian period, all trilobites became extinct.

The history of life has not been a smooth progression from simple life forms to more complex ones. No **species** lasts forever. **Evolution** is about change, and one species gives way to another that is better adapted to the surroundings. Some groups of living things, such as the dinosaurs, were extraordinarily successful. Yet individual dinosaur species still came and then vanished again. On average a species lasts between two and ten million years, and the large majority of species that have ever lived are now extinct. When a species becomes extinct, its particular combination of **genes** is removed forever from life's pool of diversity.

Many things can cause a species to become extinct. A species may die out because another species is more competitive, for example. Survival of the fittest doesn't just apply to individual members within a species, but also to species themselves. Perhaps as a result of inbreeding, a species might lack the genetic diversity to adapt to changing circumstances, such as a cooling climate or the arrival of a new predator. Many extinctions are the result of a newly evolved species replacing its ancestors, because the new species is better adapted to the environment.

Individual extinctions have occurred throughout the history of life. There is a background rate of extinction of roughly one to two species per year. However, at certain points in the past there have been mass extinctions, when many species were wiped out all at once as a result of a natural catastrophe, such as an **asteroid** strike or a major shift in the climate.

Extinction and evolution

Extinction has played a major role in the evolution of life on Earth. The **fossil** record stretching back more than 600 million years shows that there have been four or five episodes of mass extinction. The greatest known extinction episode was mentioned at the beginning of this book. It took place some 250 million years ago, at the end of the **Permian** period, when 95 percent of all marine species and 50 percent of land species were destroyed. At this time the Earth was going through a period of major geological and climate upheavals, which were probably the main cause of the extinctions.

The extinction of one species may represent an opportunity for a new species to come along and occupy the niche vacated by the vanished species. A mass extinction is an opportunity for **adaptive radiation** and the appearance of many new species. The dinosaurs began to rise to prominence after mass extinction and after the breakup of the supercontinent of **Pangea** had opened up new habitats.

Another example of a mass extinction creating new habitats for the survivors has already been discussed. The ancestors of today's mammals lived alongside the dinosaurs for tens of millions of years. All of the major gaps were filled by the dinosaurs, and the mammals could not compete with them. The first mammals were small animals that made their living as scavengers. Within 10 million years or so of the dinosaurs' extinction, all of the major **orders** of mammals (and of birds as well) had emerged. Both groups had evolved and adapted to occupy the roles that the dinosaurs had left empty.

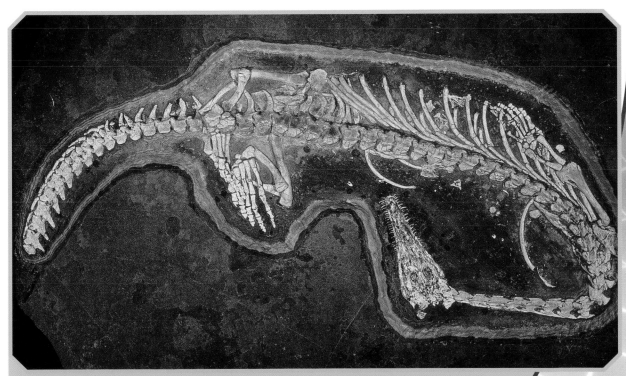

The fossilized skeleton of the aquatic reptile-like animal *Mesosaurus brazoliensis*. Extinction of many such species occurred at the end of the Permian period.

The Threat to Diversity

Roughly 12,000 years ago, North America had a spectacular variety of large animals. These included condors with a wingspan of almost 16 feet (5 meters), three types of elephants, eight types of big cats, long-legged pigs, giant wolves, and giant armadillos. There were more big animal **species** than you would find today in Africa.

Then, 11,000 years ago, 95 percent of these big animals disappeared completely. This event coincided with another major change in the area: the arrival of human beings. It may not just have been human hunters who caused these extinctions: climate change may have played a role as well. However, the speed of the extinctions, and the fact that many of the species had previously survived ice ages, suggest that it was people who tipped the balance.

A mass extinction of the Earth's organisms is under way now, and the cause of it is us, the human race. Since the invention of agriculture roughly 10,000 years ago, and with greatly increasing speed in the last 200 years, we have been changing the face of the Earth. The land and the oceans, the atmosphere, and probably the climate, have all been affected. Human activities are changing the environment and changing the conditions in which other organisms have to live. Mammals survived the catastrophe that wiped out the dinosaurs, but today more than 300 of the 4,500 or so mammal species are threatened by extinction as a result of human activity. More than two-thirds of the known bird species are threatened by the loss of their habitat. Rates of extinction are likely to continue to increas as the human **population** increases, putting greater and greater pressure on natural resources.

The Tasmanian Wolf, or thylacine (*Thylacinus cynocephalus*), is a dog-like marsupial thought to be extinct. Its numbers decreased following the introduction of dogs to Tasmania.

A modern catastrophe

Extinctions resulting from human activity have several different causes, and some are more obvious than others. Some species have been hunted to extinction. The passenger pigeon existed in large numbers in eastern North America. However, early settlers killed so many of these birds that by the end of the 19th century the population had declined from billions of birds to nearly zero. Less well known is the fact that two species of lice that were dependent on the bird became extinct as well.

A more important cause of extinctions today is the loss of habitats. Habitat destruction worldwide is taking place at a tremendous rate. The losses are greatest in tropical rainforests, where the diversity of species is also highest. More than half of these rainforests have already been cut down for timber and for farming.

This region of Costa Rica was once rainforest, but the trees have been clear-cut and now cattle graze here. Clear-cutting of rainforest could cause a mass extinction.

Another human cause of extinctions has been the introduction of non-native species into habitats. Many extinctions have taken place on islands, where species with no natural enemies are especially vulnerable to the introduction of predators such as cats and rats that are brought in either accidentally or deliberately.

The next wave

After every mass extinction that has taken place over the long history of life on Earth, diversity has increased to a greater level than before. It is sobering to think that no matter what we do we will not be able to stop life in its tracks—not even the **asteroid** that possibly shattered the dinosaurs' world could do that. There is greater diversity now than there has ever been before, but it has taken 65 million years for that diversity to evolve, which is a very long recovery time.

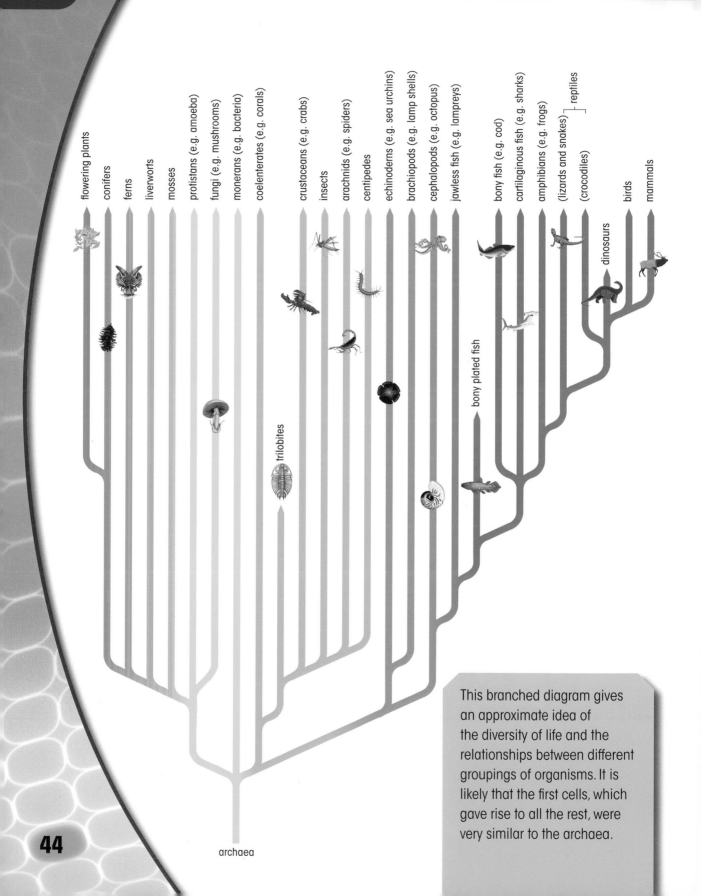

flowering plants
conifers
ferns
liverworts
mosses
protistans (e.g. amoeba)
fungi (e.g. mushrooms)
monerans (e.g. bacteria)
coelenterates (e.g. corals)
crustaceans (e.g. crabs)
insects
arachnids (e.g. spiders)
centipedes
echinoderns (e.g. sea urchins)
brachiopods (e.g. lamp shells)
cephalopods (e.g. octopus)
jawless fish (e.g. lampreys)
bony fish (e.g. cod)
cartilaginous fish (e.g. sharks)
amphibians (e.g. frogs)
(lizards and snakes) ⎤ reptiles
(crocodiles) ⎦
birds
mammals

dinosaurs

bony plated fish

trilobites

archaea

This branched diagram gives an approximate idea of the diversity of life and the relationships between different groupings of organisms. It is likely that the first cells, which gave rise to all the rest, were very similar to the archaea.

Glossary

adaptive radiation development of many different species from a single ancestral population, by adaptation to different habitats or ways of life. Adaptive radiation can occur when a population colonizes a new environment (an island, for instance), or when extinction of competing species opens up new opportunities.

algae (singular **alga**) *see* protistans

amnion membrane that encloses the embryo of reptiles, birds, and mammals

amniote animal grouping that includes the reptiles, birds, and mammals. Amniotes produce shelled eggs that contain protective structures for the embryo within. (Mammals are amniotes because the placenta is a structure evolved from the amniote egg.)

amoeba (plural **amoebae**) one of a group of single-celled, animal-like organisms that are members of the kingdom Protista

angiosperms flowering plants. The angiosperms include flowers, grasses, and some trees.

antibiotic synthetic drug or chemical produced by a micro-organism that kills bacteria. Most antibiotics are specifically effective against particular groups of bacteria.

archaea (singular **archaean**) one of two types of prokaryote organisms, the other being the bacteria. Once included as part of the bacteria kingdom, the archaea are now considered by many scientists to form a kingdom in their own right. Many of the archaea are found in extreme environments, such as near volcanic vents and in salt lakes, and for this reason they are often referred to as extremophiles.

arthropods largest phylum in the animal kingdom, containing a number of classes including crustaceans, spiders, and insects

asexual reproduction reproduction in which a single organism produces genetically identical copies (clones) of itself

asteroid piece of rock traveling through space, ranging from 0.5 to 600 miles (0.8 to 965 kilometers) in diameter

autotrophs organisms that can make their own food. Plants and many algae make their own food by photosynthesis.

bacteria diverse group of organisms that are found in almost every part of the Earth. Some can make their own food using light energy, others use chemical energy.

binomial nomenclature the scientific naming of organisms with a two-part Latin name, the first part indicating the organism's genus, the second its species

bryophyta (**bryophytes**) phylum (division) of small, simple, rootless plants that includes the mosses and liverworts

Cambrian geological period of time, 545 to 505 million years ago, during which there was a sudden explosion of large animal fossils

carbohydrate chemical compound composed of carbon, hydrogen, and oxygen. Glucose is a simple carbohydrate.

Carnivora (**carnivores**) carnivore is a general term for any meat-eating organism. The order Carnivora is a specific group of meat-eating mammals that includes cats, dogs, bears, and seals.

cartilage stiff material, more flexible than bone, that is used as a supporting tissue in vertebrates. Some vertebrates (such as sharks) have skeletons entirely made of cartilage, rather than bone.

chloroplast organelle found within plant cells where photosynthesis takes place

class in the classification of living things, a class is a grouping of organisms that is larger than an order but smaller than a phylum

cyanobacteria (also known as blue greens) single-celled or filamentous prokaryotes that carry out photosynthesis

cytoplasm all of the contents of a cell between the nucleus and the outer membrane

denticles tiny, toothlike structures that cover the skin of sharks and other cartilaginous fish. The denticles make the skin feel like sandpaper.

dicotyledons angiosperms that have two cotyledons (seed leaves) in the embryo. Plants such as roses, beans, and oak trees are dicotyledons.

DNA (deoxyribonucleic acid) genetic material of living things. DNA carries instructions for constructing, maintaining, and reproducing living cells.

embryo very young organism in the early stages of development, before it emerges from the egg or seed, or is born from its mother's uterus

enzyme special proteins that control the speed of chemical reactions within the cell. Each reaction has its own specific enzyme.

eukaryote one of the two basic types of living cell. Eukaryote cells contain structures within them, such as the nucleus. All living things except the archaea and bacteria are eukaryotes.

evolution changes in groups of organisms over many generations, by which they adapt to their environment and form new species

family in the classification of living things, a family is a grouping of organisms that is bigger than a genus but smaller than an order

food chain organisms linked in a relationship by the foods they eat. For instance, rabbits eat grass, and are themselves eaten by predators such as foxes. Grass, rabbits, and foxes together form a food chain.

fossil organism, part of an organism, or traces of an organism preserved in rocks

gene section of DNA coding for a single protein or part of a protein. Genes are the basic units of heredity, through which the characteristics of organisms are passed on from generation to generation.

Glossary

genetic material substance called DNA, found within each living cell, which carries the means for creating a new organism. This genetic material is passed on from generation to generation.

genus (plural **genera**) in the classification of living things, a genus is a grouping of organisms that is larger than a species but smaller than a family

gymnosperma (**gymnosperms**) phylum (division) of plants that includes conifer trees such as pines, spruces, and firs

herbivore animal that feeds only on plants

heterotroph organism that needs an external source of food to survive. All animals are heterotrophs.

hornworts simple, green, leaflike plants similar to liverworts. They belong to the phylum Bryophyta.

hyphae (singular **hypha**) thin, threadlike structures that form the body (mycelium) of a fungus

kingdom in the classification of living things, the largest grouping of organisms. Most classification systems divide the living world into five, sometimes six, kingdoms.

lichen plant-like growths covering other plants or rocks

lignin tough, waterproof material found in the thickened cell walls of some plant cells. These lignified cells give land plants the rigidity they need to support themselves.

lipids oils, fats, waxes, and other fatty substances found in living cells

liverworts small, simple, leaflike plants found in wet places such as river banks and damp woods. Liverworts are bryophytes.

minerals simple chemical substances required by living organisms to function healthily. Plants get minerals from the soil, animals get minerals in their food.

monocotyledons plants that have one seed leaf. The leaves often have parallel veins. Species include grasses, onions, orchids, and palm trees.

monotremes sub-class of primitive, egg-laying mammals such as platypuses and echidnas

mutation random change in an organism's genetic material. Mutations can produce new characteristics in organisms and are an important factor in evolution.

mycelium body of a fungus, consisting of a network of threadlike hyphae

nucleus in biology, a large organelle found in eukaryote cells, which contains the cell's genetic material

omnivore animal that eats plants and other animals

order in the classification of living things, an order is a grouping of organisms that is larger than a family but smaller than a class

organ collection of different tissues in an animal's body that work together to carry out a particular function, such as the heart, which pumps blood throughout the body.

organelle one of several different structures, surrounded by a membrane, found in eukaryote cells. The cell nucleus and plant chloroplast are two types of organelle.

organic anything related to or derived from living things. Organic compounds are carbon-containing chemicals found in living things.

Pangea supercontinent formed from all the present continents before they broke apart

parasite organism that lives in or on another organism, obtaining food from it without giving anything in return

Permian geological period of time, between 290 million and 250 million years ago. The end of this period is marked by the Permian extinction, in which 95 percent of all marine animals died out.

photosynthesis process by which plants and algae make sugary food using energy from sunlight, carbon dioxide from the air, and water

phylum (plural **phyla**) in the classification of living things, a phylum is the largest grouping of organisms within a kingdom

placenta structure that forms in the uterus (womb) of pregnant mammals. It nourishes the embryo as it grows.

plasmid small, circular piece of DNA found in bacterial cells. Plasmids often contain a gene or genes that give resistance to an antibiotic.

population in biology, a population is a group of organisms within a species that live together in a particular area

Precambrian geological period before the Cambrian, from about 4 billion years ago to 545 million years ago

prokaryote simplest type of living cell. All living things except the archaea and bacteria are eukaryotes.

proteins substances that make up many cell structures and control a cell's reactions. Proteins are large molecules made up of many subunits called amino acids.

protistans kingdom of eukaryote organisms, mostly single-celled. Some protistans have animal-like qualities (protozoans), while others are more like plants (algae).

protozoan *see* protistans

respiration process by which all organisms obtain energy from food, by breaking down sugars into simpler substances. Anaerobic respiration can take place without oxygen. Aerobic respiration is a much more efficient process that requires oxygen to work.

sexual reproduction form of reproduction in which sex cells from two parents, the father and the mother, combine to form a cell that will grow into a new individual

species basic unit of classification—a group of closely related living things that can breed together and produce fertile offspring

symbiotic any close relationship between two or more different species of organisms, such as flowering plants and pollinating insects

taxonomy study of the classification of organisms

tetrapods any four-limbed vertebrate, such as amphibians, reptiles, birds, and mammals

tissue in biology, a group of similar cells that have a specific function in an organism. Examples are muscle and nerve tissue.

vascular system system of tubular cells or vessels that carry water and food around a plant or animal

Further Reading and Websites

Books

Anderson, Bridget. *The Kingdoms of Life: Classification.* Hong Kong: Lickle, 2003.

Spillsbury, Richard and Louise. *Plant Classification.* Chicago: Heinemann Library, 2003.

Wallace, Holly. *Life Processes: Classification.* Chicago: Heinemann Library, 2006.

Websites

Animal Diversity Web (http://animaldiversity.ummz.umich.edu/site/index.html)
    A searchable database of the Kingdom Animalia.

Flowering Plant Diversity (http://scitec.uwichill.edu.bb/bcs/bl14apl/flow2.htm)
    An introduction to the world of flowering plants.

University of California Museum of Paleontology
    (www.ucmp.berkeley.edu/exhibits/historyoflife.php)
    An introduction to life on Earth from 3.7 billion years ago until now.

Index